Scriptural Delights

Exploring Psalm 119

Scriptural Delights

Exploring Psalm 119

by

Jim Harris

&

Dave Roberts

Acknowledgements

Editing & Proofing: Roger Kirby

Scriptural Delight – version 1.0

Text & Graphics Copyright © 2015 Dave Roberts

ISBN-13: 978-1507624203 (CreateSpace-Assigned)
ISBN-10: 1507624204

This has previously been released as Podcasts on the Partakers website: http://www.partakers.co.uk

Dedication

Firstly to the Lord our God – Father, Son and Holy Spirit. I would not be here without Him and I know that He loves me.

Secondly to my wife, Youngmi. She is my one and my only. I can't imagine life without her. I thank God for her – she makes me laugh and smile – even when I am in the midst of trouble.

To a lady now with the Lord – Rose. She is now more alive than any of us on this earth. She was like a mother to me and I know she took great delight in God who was her refuge and delighted in reading His word.

How to look up the Bible

Book of the Bible. In this case, the book of Luke. Dont be afraid to look at the contents page to find it. We all do it, even if we don't want to admit it!

This is the Verse of the Chapter. In this case, it is verse 9. Think of it as a sentence or part of a sentence.

This is the chapter of the book. In this case, Chapter 19.

Contents

Introduction

(Dave Roberts)

Psalm 119, with all its rigours, tests and temptations to stop reading because of its length, has a vibrant beauty and many pearls of wisdom to offer Christians living in the twenty first century. There is some repetition in both the Psalm and the comments we have written. They are inevitable I think, in such a long poem on one subject.

Why did the Psalmist write this piece of poetic majesty? I think it was to encourage followers of God to lead a holy life, a life of obedient godliness, and to show what true worship of God is like through the study of His written word. To help the reader memorise Psalm 119 in the original Hebrew it is written as an alphabetical acrostic.

There are 22 stanzas in the psalm, each consisting of eight lines. In Hebrew the first letter in all eight lines of the first stanza is Aleph, the first letter of the Hebrew alphabet. In the second stanza the first letter in all eight lines is Beth, the second letter of the alphabet. This continues all the way through the Hebrew alphabet until the twenty second stanza, which begins with the letter Taw, the final letter of the alphabet. It would be like writing a poem that begins:

> A good boy eats apples
> Apples that are rosy red
> Blue skies are lovely
> Bright skies are warm

Now, while all that may be very good for helping memorizing Psalm 119 in Hebrew, in English it does not translate like that, as you can see just by looking at it. That doesn't mean we shouldn't try to memorize it though. Despite its length and its seemingly repetitive composition, it is indeed an unparalleled work of beauty, colour and descriptiveness.

Words for Scripture

Throughout Psalm 119, the writer, the Psalmit, has eight different words for Scripture or Law of the Lord. When the Psalmist says God's Law, Law of the Lord or Torah, he does not mean, as some think, just the Mosaic Law, but rather all of the revealed will and mind of God in the Old Testament scriptures.

We, of course, don't know how much of the Old Testament was written when the Psalmist was writing Psalm 119, but we do know that he would have had at his disposal at least the first five books - Genesis, Exodus, Leviticus and Deuteronomy to you and me. It is also quite probable he had access to some of the historical books and maybe even the book of Job.

Here in Psalm 119, the Psalmist uses eight key words about God's revealed word, both to bring some variety into what he says and to highlight the different ways in which the Lord speaks to us. For those the Psalmist wrote to in the first place, this meant the Pentateuch and some of the rest of the Old Testament. For us today it is the hugely more exciting writings of the New Testament. It is quite right and proper to take these later writings in this way because they are all the Word of the Lord. Are you ready to explore Psalm 119?

So with that brief introduction let's investigate these eight words. Unfortunately not all the translations use the same English words to translate the originals. We are going to stick by the words of the NIV. One other important thing to note is that the Psalmist clearly takes a very open and fresh view of the part of the Bible he has. He repeatedly asks to be taught what it means, to be given understanding, to have the Lord speak to him very directly through the parts of the Bible the Psalmist has available to him. Of course, this is a very good lesson for us. Sometimes we like to regard the Bible we have as only a gloriously comprehensive list of commands, orders, exhortations etc. Rather we should see the Bible as a window into an ever deeper relationship with the Lord as He speaks to us through our reading and studying of it.

1. Law (v1): Law is the most common of all the words used here in Psalm 119. It has as its foundation the word teach or direction and can be synonymous with one commandment or a whole book of laws to be followed. It shows that God's revealed will is not simply for observation only but is primarily for obedience. The Jews in New Testament times thought the first 5 books of the Bible as the pre-eminent Law.

2. Statutes or decrees (verse 2): When the Psalmist speaks of statutes, he writes about the permanence of Scripture, as an enduring reminder of the Lord and His goodness.

3. Precepts (verse 4): This word is drawn from a person who is looking into a situation and getting ready to act. This word reflects specific instructions as told by the Lord.

4. Decrees or statutes (verse 5): This means that what God says is a reliable witness, a witness that is faithful, dependable and true. Rules and high standards that are given by God, are for living a highly practical and obedient godly life with warnings against disobedience abound within this expression.

5. Commands (verse 6): This word, command, signifies a direct order from authority. It is not simply power to influence but rather the right to give orders and an attitude of assuredness.

6. Laws (verse 7): This word is a plural, and therefore different from the 'Law'. Within the Old Testament, this would be judgements or decisions as laid down by a supremely wise Judge. It is more than judgements, as it signifies the justice of being dutiful and responsible.

7. Word (verse 9): This the most popular expression used by the Psalmist, it simply means God's revealed truth in any shape, form, commandment or statement.

8. Word or Promise (verses 11 & 38): Unfortunately translated two ways in the NIV, its root or foundation is from 'to say' or 'promise to do or say'. God's promises are true and He always keeps His promises.

Stanza 1. Aleph

(Dave Roberts)

[1] Blessed are those whose ways are blameless,
who walk according to the law of the LORD.
[2] Blessed are those who keep his statutes
and seek him with all their heart -
[3] they do no wrong;
but follow his ways.
[4] You have laid down precepts
that are to be fully obeyed.

[5] Oh, that my ways were steadfast
in obeying your decrees.
[6] Then I would not be put to shame
when I consider all your commands.
[7] I will praise you with an upright heart
as I learn your righteous laws.
[8] I will obey your decrees;
do not utterly forsake me.

What do you regard as being successful in life? Is it the amount of money in your bank accounts? Or perhaps it is a long and successful career? Now, while there is nothing essentially wrong with those sorts of things, the Psalmist writes that the key to living a successful life is to be obedient to God and doing, as He has decreed. God has spoken and given His decrees, law, commands and statutes.

Look at the picture the Psalmist paints. Walk according to the Law of the Lord - keep His statutes. Seek Him wholeheartedly. The person who is blessed doesn't do wrong against other people (that is what is meant in verse 3) and is obedient to God's decrees. The truly successful person considers how best to apply God's commands in their life, letting them permeate every facet of their being.

A truly successful life is one, which is utterly obedient to God and God's commands, precepts and decrees. Not only in the doing of them, but also in the underlying attitude. God's commands are not only things to be done, but also about things not to be done. When we sin, and we all do, sometimes, it is because we do something that is wrong and contrary to God's law. But there are also sins that are the things that we do not do when God has commanded that we should do them.

That is simply disobedience. God's commands, it should be noted, are not to become objects of worship themselves. God alone, the giver of the commands, is to be worshipped and adored.

Some people I meet are all for the laws of God but forget about the law-giver, Almighty God. God, as revealed in the Bible, is to be followed with commitment but also with consistency or as the Psalmist says "steadfastly". Obedience to God brings about praise to God and does not end in disappointment or shame to the disciple. Obedience brings joy and a glow to the face.

How can we be fully obedient to God? Can we through our own strength, wisdom and actions fully satisfy all of God's laws? By no means. The reason being is that we will undoubtedly fail if we try to obey God in our own strength. Read verse 8 again. God will help you to fulfil all His commands if you ask Him. God will not abandon or forsake you, but wants to help. God is personal, and not distant – He will help. Amazing.

To have a truly successful life is to be obedient to God and His decrees, cries the Psalmist. What has all this to do with the Christian in the twenty first century?

Jesus Christ is the only man who ever fully obeyed God in every facet of life. He was the only man to be truly successful and by claiming Him as our God, then we too can be successful. If you need help to be obedient, just ask Him. If you are a Christian, you have God inside you through the person of the Holy Spirit.

Part of His role in your life is to guide you and help you to live a life of obedience to Jesus Christ the Son, so that the praise, honour and glory go to God the Father. Will you ask the Holy Spirit to do that for you? Will you "keep in step with the Spirit" as Paul expressed it in Galatians 5:25? If you have done wrong, ask God for forgiveness of that sin and do not let it trap you in its snare. Be quick to ask forgiveness and do not fall for the tempter's traps. Be blessed by God, and to show that you are blessed, live a life of obedience to Him.

Stanza 2. Beth

(Dave Roberts)

9 How can a young person stay on the path of purity?

By living according to your word.

10 I seek you with all my heart;

do not let me stray from your commands.

11 I have hidden your word in my heart

that I might not sin against you.

12 Praise be to you, LORD;

teach me your decrees.

13 With my lips I recount

all the laws that come from your mouth.

14 I rejoice in following your statutes

as one rejoices in great riches.

15 I meditate on your precepts

and consider your ways.

16 I delight in your decrees;

I will not neglect your word.

From verse 9, it would seem that the young 'person' is the Psalmist himself. Older versions say 'man'. (We want to use the latest NIV but this brings the problem of using inclusive language. To do so all the way through will be difficult and often clumsy compared with assuming that the Psalmist was a man – as in those days and in that culture, he almost certainly was. So with apologies to all ladies reading this we will stick with 'he' and 'him' etc. all the way through.

He is seeking wholeheartedly a way to keep himself pure and upright before God. He is striving most earnestly not to stray from obeying God and God's commands. The commands are so embedded within him that they form part of his very being, such is this young man's desire not to sin against the Lord. He then goes on to complete this section, celebrating with great joy the virtues of God's Word, commands and laws. He is full of praise because God teaches him. He rejoices at the joy he experiences in following God and being obedient to Him. He meditates, reflects and contemplates God's ways and promises not to neglect God and God's promises.

Where in verse 11 he says "word", the better translation is "promise", which is number 8 in our list of meanings in the second of this series. He will keep

God's promises within himself as a reminder of God's goodness and holiness. It is a reminder to us all when we are struggling with some aspect of faith to remember God's promise to us. When the evil one comes knocking and says that God has abandoned you, remember that God has not abandoned you, will not abandon you and always has a grip on you.

The Psalmist describes the benefits of reading and meditating upon the Bible. God's words become a delight as he follows God's decrees. A sense of wonder is instilled as he meditates on God's word. Strength overcomes tiredness as he listens to God speaking through the Bible. All these things are also true for the Christian disciple. The promises of God stand firm for all time and they are trustworthy. God is both capable of trusting a human being and can be completely trusted by a human being.

The Psalmist would be familiar with the Covenant God had made with Moses and the commandments that were given so they would know how to relate socially to God. He would remember that the decrees dictated their religious life so that God could be approached by humanity on His terms. And for all that, the Psalmist knew that salvation was from God's grace and not through blind obedience to a list of rules.

In Jesus Christ, you have His promises written on your heart if you are a follower of Him. As a follower of Jesus Christ, you have God the Holy Spirit within you. When you are struggling, ask Him for help. Read your Bible faithfully and consistently, all of it – not just the favourite parts. God the Holy Spirit will remind you of things contained within it, just when you need it or need to give that insight to another person.

Remember key Bible verses and use them to be obedient to Him and to lovingly direct others to be obedient to Him. We need to feed our minds with that which is pure, and then it will be easier to control our thought lives. There is an old computer industry saying, that if you put garbage in, you will get garbage out. Thoughts come from the outside, it is what you do with the thought that matters. Sinful desires often start out as thoughts and are easily inflamed, played upon and can grow remarkably quickly. Do you have an area of your life where you are particularly vulnerable to disobeying God? Then learn what God has to say in the Bible about that area of life, and memorise some verses about it. Jesus Christ, the only person ever to live a fully obedient life to God, used the Scriptures constantly. We can do likewise, because if we are followers of Jesus Christ, we have God the Holy Spirit inside us to help us recall what we have read and endeavoured to memorise.

Stanza 3. Gimel

(Dave Roberts)

[17] Be good to your servant, while I live;
that I may obey your word.
[18] Open my eyes that I may see
wonderful things in your law.
[19] I am a stranger on earth;
do not hide your commands from me.
[20] My soul is consumed with longing
for your laws at all times.

[21] You rebuke the arrogant, who are accursed,
those who stray from your commands.
[22] Remove from me their scorn and contempt,
for I keep your statutes.
[23] Though rulers sit together and slander me,
your servant will meditate on your decrees.
[24] Your statutes are my delight;
they are my counsellors.

The Psalmist's plea in verse 17 is not an uncommon one in the Old Testament. The Psalmist is turning his eyes away from his own situation, and onto God and what God wants from him – total obedience. Now it could be that the Psalmist's life was in danger of physical death from one of his enemies. Indeed right through the psalm it is clear that he did not have an easy life but was constantly challenged about his faith. It is equally true that the Psalmist is also speaking of his spiritual life, which is only in fellowship with God.

Salvation was not and is not through keeping the rules of the Law. The Law originally given to the people of God after they had been redeemed from Egypt and had started on their journey of faith, was there to show the futility of man's efforts to save himself and walk properly in the way of faith.

Salvation could only come from God alone, which it would do through the Messiah who was to come. It was due to God's mercy that the Psalmist had fellowship with him so the Psalmist wants to offer himself in total obedience to God. Verse 18 shows this, because when the Psalmist sees the beauty of the Law, he realizes God does wondrous things. It is as if scales or cataracts fall from his eyes so that he can see clearly. Once he was blind, but now he can see.

The Psalmist earnestly seeks to serve God, because it is due to God alone that he has spiritual life, indeed any life at all. The Psalmist continues to build up metaphors about his relationship with God through His commands, laws, statutes and decrees. Truly the Psalmist sees obedience to God as of the highest importance, the only worthy response to God's grace and mercy towards him, or anybody.

For if obedience is worship, the Psalmist is keen to make his life a life of total worship to God. The Psalmist recognizes that life on earth is only temporary, that is why he calls himself a stranger on earth (v19). There is a better place for him and only God can provide the way there, through His grace and mercy. Thinking about it was a relief from the worries and strains the Psalmist was enduring. Despite all that's going on around him, as he notes in v23 where other rulers plot against him (thus suggesting he moved in quite senior circles, perhaps as a court adviser), he puts his hope in God alone.

The Psalmist is concerned that he might become arrogant and proud because of his awareness of being in touch with the Lord through his concern for God's laws and obeying Him. It is in humility that the Psalmist maintains his fellowship with God. Aware that many things may distract him, the Psalmist occupies himself with the reading of the Law and being in communion with God alone. By seeking the counsel of God through Scripture, the Psalmist's worries disappear because his eyes turn towards God and away from the problems.

God is the solution to problems; following God, obeying God and walking with God are the Psalmist priorities. The promises of God are a sweet healing ointment to a troubled soul and a fragrantly pleasing aroma to the senses. The Psalmist knows that reading Scripture and obeying God through it, provides a stable relationship between himself and God.

When Jesus says "Do not worry…" (Matthew 6:25-34), he stipulates that we are to seek God's righteousness and be dependent upon God to supply all our needs. Let tomorrow worry about itself, Jesus said, and seek God at all opportunity.

Remember who you are, he says. You are of infinite worth to God, much more than plants and animals. Allow God to permeate every aspect of your life and let God be seen in every aspect of your life. An essential part of seeking God's righteousness is reading the Bible and seeing how He guides and speaks into individual situations. For the Psalmist, God's words were his counsel. Are they yours?

What worries and concerns have you got today? Ask God to help you and ask others to ask God on your behalf. By asking, you show humility and dependence upon God. As humans, we are born dependent on God and others as babies and children. Then as we grow through life, we are in more subtle and much less obvious ways still dependent upon God for all things and dependent upon other people as well. By showing our need to be helped by other people and dependence upon them, we show our need and dependence upon God.

Jesus Christ exemplified that. As a baby he was dependent on milk from his mother and to have his bottom wiped. In dying, when he was on the cross he was dependent on others to offer him a drink. In his death he was dependent upon God the Father to raise him to life again, just as He had promised to do. Three days later, Jesus rose from the tomb of death to new life. God is totally reliable and will help you when you ask. Maybe not in the way you expect, but due to His mercy and grace, He who is the wisest of all, will help you in the best way possible. God has promised and He always keeps his promises.

Stanza 4. Daleth

(Dave Roberts)

[25] I am laid low in the dust;

preserve my life according to your word.

[26] I gave an account of my ways and you answered me;

teach me your decrees.

[27] Cause me to understand the way of your precepts;

that I may meditate on your wonderful deeds.

[28] My soul is weary with sorrow;

strengthen me according to your word.

[29] Keep me from deceitful ways;

be gracious to me and teach me your law.

[30] I have chosen the way of faithfulness;

I have set my heart on your laws.

[31] I hold fast to your statutes, LORD;

do not let me be put to shame.

[32] I run in the path of your commands,

for you have broadened my understanding.

From verse 25, the Psalmist describes himself and the condition he is in. He is laid low, weary and tired. He is in desperate straits, heavily burdened and clinging onto life, both spiritually and physically. He is at the bottom of a pit and the only way out is up. So what does he do? He cries out a series of short prayers to God. Revive me. Preserve me. Make me live again. O God, my Lord, you promised that you would restore me again to yourself. He may be low, but he knows that God will answer him. The Psalmist knows that God's testimonies about Himself are true. The Psalmist knows that God's decrees, precepts, commands and statutes are glorious, and that through them, he can be set free.

The Psalmist piles up the metaphors about God's Law or Word and his own response to them. He is never negative about any aspect of God's Law because he knows that the Law is his only hope of knowing God and confirming his expectation God will rescue him from both physical and spiritual death. He knows that to live a life of obedience to God, he needs to read about God's commands, precepts and interactions with those in the past.

Remember, the Psalmist would have had at least the first 5 books of the Bible at his disposal: Genesis, Exodus, Leviticus, Numbers and Deuteronomy as the

Canon of the Old Testament had not been settled at his time. The Psalmist has a choice to make. He could just wallow in self-pity and curl up and die. But he doesn't.

In verse 30, he makes a conscious decision to follow God, hold fast to God and run with God. That is not the usual action of somebody who is wearied and burdened. God has answered his prayers and restored him, just as He promised to do. God is faithful. What was the catalyst for this? Verse 29 says that God's graciousness is seen in the Law. The only time God's commandments and the Law are a bad thing is when it is used as a means to salvation. God's Law was never meant to be as a means to salvation, only to show how foolish it was to seek salvation that way and that salvation is only due to God's mercy and God's grace. Through God's gracious Law, the Psalmist has renewed energy and is able to fly once more with God. God's revealing of Himself and His rescue/restoration go together.

What we are reading about here is something often forgotten in the modern church. Christian faith is about faithfulness – the same word is used for both faith and faithfulness in the New Testament. It is not just about being 'born again'. If a new-born baby stays a baby and never grows there is something seriously wrong with it.

Exactly the same is true of a second born person. They need to grow or there is something seriously wrong with them. That is why the Psalmist is so keen to grow himself. So he is desperate to be taught the way of the Lord, to 'run in the path', through the law, the statutes and the commands of the Lord.

Jesus also echoes this when He proclaims: "Come to me, all you who are weary and burdened, and I will give you rest. Take my yoke upon you and learn from me, for I am gentle and humble in heart, and you will find rest for your souls. For my yoke is easy and my burden is light." (Matthew 11:28-30) Why is Jesus saying this?

Firstly to those undergoing the burden of religion as many of the Jewish people did at the time, under the regime of the Pharisees and the Jewish leaders – people were spiritually oppressed by the use of the Law as a spiritual obligation requiring them to conform to the extended version of the Law imposed by the scholars. Religiosity had become more important than 'the way of faithfulness' and 'running in the path of your commands' – the things that the Psalmist desired to do so earnestly.

Secondly Jesus is saying this to those who are

searching for God, that if they do so wholeheartedly and expectantly, then they will find Him. The Greeks had long carried out an exhausted search for truth. Whether it was the search for divine truth or the unnecessary burden of religion, Jesus came to set people free – free from their burdens. In some ways living the life of a Christian is difficult, but not as a religious obligation. Following Jesus can be hard work if we try to do it in our own strength. But if we do it in the strength of the Holy Spirit who lives inside us if we are Christian, then the burden is light and the yoke is easy.

So if you are struggling under some burden of man-made religion or seeking truth, then look no further than Jesus, who claimed to be God and was God. Are you struggling to live the Christian life in your own strength and not the strength of God the Holy Spirit who lives inside you? How, this very day, can this God ease your burdens, lighten your load and restore you to Himself? Ask Jesus to take the burden you or others have placed upon yourself and restore you once more so that like the Psalmist you can follow, hold and run.

Stanza 5. He

(Dave Roberts)

[33] Teach me, LORD, the way of your decrees;
that I may follow it to the end.
[34] Give me understanding, so that I may keep your law
and obey it with all my heart.
[35] Direct me in the path of your commands,
for there I find delight.
[36] Turn my heart toward your statutes
and not toward selfish gain.

[37] Turn my eyes away from worthless things;
preserve my life according to your word.
[38] Fulfil your promise to your servant,
so that you may be feared.
[39] Take away the disgrace I dread,
for your laws are good.
[40] How I long for your precepts.
In your righteousness preserve my life.

Having being revived in the previous section, the Psalmist now seeks to be taught. He continues using words for the Law such as decrees, commands, statutes and precepts. His responses are equally clear: Teachable, kept, obedient, directed, turned and yearned. His initial outburst from the first verse is a heartfelt cry "Teach me to follow your decrees O Great God so that I will discover my reward." He then goes from the desire for teaching to one for understanding, because understanding is the practical application of what has been taught to his life as a believer.

Obedience is the result for the Psalmist through applying and understanding what God has taught him. This obedience then is the catalyst for the next part – direction. If the Psalmist moves in obedience, then God Himself will direct him. Something that is moving, and not standing still, can be easily steered. When Almighty God using His decrees, directs the Psalmist, the Psalmist finds true ecstasy, joy and delight.

True happiness comes from serving God and obeying Him by serving others. The Psalmist does all this, not for a feel good factor or for his own pride and self-righteousness. No. The Psalmist does this so his life is preserved, abandoning all that is worthless, in pursuit of that which is eternally worthwhile. If his own work of selfishness is useless, what does the Psalmist say about the work of the Lord? The Lord's work is the fulfilment of His promise to the Psalmist – to preserve his life in the Lord's righteousness.

Righteousness under the Mosaic covenant was active obedience to God and living according to God's ways. How is it that the Psalmist is declared righteous? By fearing the Lord (v38) and when the Lord is feared, then the utter disgrace of disobedience is taken away. God fulfils His promises always. There is a battle ensuing within the Psalmist – the inner battle where he can choose between two ways to live. First is the choice to live in obedience to God. Secondly he can choose to disobey God and live life his own selfish way. By choosing to obey God, the Psalmist is preserved.

What does this have to do with us as twenty-first century Christians? The Christian life is to be an active one of dynamic contact with the Holy Spirit who lives with and within us. Sometimes we like to think our own self-righteousness is what is going to save us. We all think that at some point even if we are not aware of it. When we do that, we are no better than the Pharisees of Jesus' time. The Pharisees were righteous people, but they were looking to their own righteousness for salvation. They adapted the Laws of God for their own ends. Jesus said that unless one's righteousness exceeds that of the Pharisees, then we can't be saved. How is that possible? It is possible, because true righteousness is not an external righteousness like that of the Pharisees, but an internal righteousness – a righteousness of the heart. A righteousness which will see God the Holy Spirit living within those who accept Jesus Christ as Lord and Saviour, and so have the laws of God written on their hearts.

The Pharisees had a distorted view of the Law imagining it was about external obedience. But as the Psalmist here reminds us, the "obedience of the heart" (v34) shows it also has to be an internal matter as well. Righteousness under the New Covenant, is not just an active external obedience to God but an internal avowal before Him. How is this internal righteousness seen? It is as the Apostle Paul would write in Philippians 2:12-13: "…continue to work out your salvation with fear and trembling, for it is God who works in you to will and to act in order to fulfil his good purpose."

When God the Father sees you, if you are a Christian, he sees the righteousness of Jesus Christ His Son. When Jesus died on the cross, it was so that all who chose to follow Him could be declared righteous and wear the robe of righteousness. As a Christian, you have the righteousness of Jesus Christ (Ephesians 1:7; Acts 13:38-39; Romans 3:22) and you have received the gift of righteousness (Romans 5:17) through faith in Jesus Christ (Philippians 3:9). If you need help in any area of your life, then ask God the Holy Spirit, who lives inside you, to help you. He will, because God the Holy Spirit is in the transformation business.

What areas of your life do you need to hand control over to Him? We all have areas to work on, ceding control and handing them to God. How are you doing at living as a Christian? Are you struggling in some area of life where that specific aspect of your life is in direct disobedience to God? That is the pursuit of your own selfish gain, as the Psalmist would say. Ask for help, and He will help.

Stanza 6. Waw

(Dave Roberts)

41. May your unfailing love come to me, Lord,
your salvation, according to your promise;
42. then I can answer anyone who taunts me,
for I trust in your word.
43. Never take your word of truth from my mouth,
for I have put my hope in your laws.
44. I will always obey your law,
for ever and ever.
45. I will walk about in freedom,
for I have sought out your precepts.
46. I will speak of your statutes before kings
and will not be put to shame,
47. for I delight in your commands
because I love them.
48. I reach out for your commands, which I love,
that I may meditate on your decrees.

The Psalmist seems to know have a recap of all that he has said so far. The reason I say that, is because each verse in the original language starts with 'and', (which means it must have been the easiest stanza to write.) In the previous sections, the Psalmist declares the amazing blessings of God, the faithful promises of God, the total obedience demanded by God, the invigorating testimonies of God and then the glorious teachings of God. God's Word is utterly amazing and shown to be a breath-taking adventure. After all that adventure, this recap point is like a love letter back to God.

These 8 verses are a response to the love of God and His word. The Psalmist starts out by praising God, because God has promised him salvation. God's promises are true, kind and unfailing. God is mighty to save and saves mightily. If God has said it, He will do it. But how does God promise salvation? God promises salvation through His unfailing love, kindness and tender mercy. That is why the Psalmist puts the cause before the effect. Salvation can be attained by no other means, but only through God's mercy and grace – God's twin wellsprings working in unison.

Next, the Psalmist deals with those who disagree with God's plans and promises. What happens when scoffers come to taunt? Well, the Psalmist in verse 42 replies that God's word is true, it is trustworthy and His word never disappoints or dismays. Scoffers can come from within the Church as well as those outside. This doesn't matter a jot. God's word is still true. Not blindly trustworthy, but verifiably trustworthy evidentially and experientially. So enamoured is the Psalmist with all the facets of God's Word, that he never wants its truth to depart from him and he wants always to speak God's truth.

WOW. His heart is full of desire of God and for God that he cannot help but talk about God and God's mercy and grace. Due to salvation, the Psalmist's hope is in God alone and because of that hope he will be obedient to God in all ways forever. Because of the obedience that is the outworking of his salvation, the Psalmist can walk through life safely and freely. When troubles come to ensnare him, he will be able to deal with them effectively because his mind will be controlled and his demeanour, or manner, calm. God will guide him through the storms and harassment as the Psalmist studies and recalls God's words.

Being in possession of God's wisdom in dealing with troubles, the Psalmist is again free to speak about them to anybody, even kings. Not only will he speak against the scoffers but even to leaders –anybody and everybody. It is from the heart that he speaks without shame or embarrassment, of God's mercy and grace as revealed in God's word. And why does he do this? He does this because again, he loves to read and hear of God and God's commands (v47). This delight is an intense desire and actively expressed love.

Verse 48 shows the Psalmist reaching out. He is holding his hands up and out in an act of reverence, prayer and worship. This act springs out from knowing that when he reads, studies, cogitates, meditates and thinks of all of God's word, he is getting to know His God and Saviour more intimately and deepening his relationship with Almighty God. You can feel the passion oozing out of him. There is a deep yearning in the Psalmist to see how God reveals Himself through the Scriptures, the Law, through His dealings with people. All this as a result of 'and', as he looks back on what he has written previously.

How are you doing with your Bible reading? How are you letting what you read permeate every facet of your life as you allow the Holy Spirit to reveal God's commands and guidance to you? What are you basing your salvation on? Scripture says salvation is to be found only through God's grace and mercy exhibited by God the Son on the cross. Do not be fooled by scoffers or the enemy, satan, into thinking otherwise. Delight yourself in reading your Bible and showing your salvation by obeying what God says in it. Speak freely of God and His dealings with you without embarrassment or shame. Know He is in charge and that He will help you, no matter what you are going through or circumstance you find yourself in. Ask for help, and He will help. He has promised and He will do it.

Stanza 7. Zayin

(Dave Roberts)

[49] Remember your word to your servant,
for you have given me hope.
[50] My comfort in my suffering is this:
Your promise preserves my life.
[51] The arrogant mock me unmercifully,
but I do not turn from your law.
[52] I remember, LORD, your ancient laws,
and I find comfort in them.
[53] Indignation grips me because of the wicked,
who have forsaken your law.
[54] Your decrees are the theme of my song
wherever I lodge.
[55] In the night, LORD, I remember your name,
that I may keep your law.
[56] This has been my practice:
I obey your precepts.

In the previous section, the Psalmist did a recap – a summary section of what has gone before. Now he proceeds to the dual role of memory in the life of the servant of God – as both the one being reminded and the one who remembers. The Psalmist is under pressure and is enduring great suffering. He is being mocked, scorned and ridiculed relentlessly by his opponents. Where is his comfort and consolation coming from? What is his reaction to opposition? He is full of hope even though he is going through all of this

The Psalmist is still full of hope because he knows He knows that God will fulfil his promises to him, and therefore he has a confident hope in the God of his salvation. So, the Psalmist finds great consolation and comfort in bringing to mind what God reminds him of in His word. The Psalmist knows God's promises preserve and sustain him in times of trouble.

Therefore, despite the arrogance of his persecutors, the Psalmist continues to obey God and follow His Law and commands. The Psalmist values his integrity before God as being more important than giving into the demands of those who seek to destroy him. Having been reminded by the Lord and having reflected on Him, His Law and His Word, it is time for action: and the act is that of remembering. We can only remember something if we make some effort, perhaps some great effort, to get it into our minds. As we have seen in this Psalm, in relation to God's word, the Psalmist has read it faithfully, systematically and methodically. Repeating it to himself, so that when times of trouble come, he can remember it easily.

When times of injustice such as v53 talks about came, he became very zealous for God against the law-breakers. Not only that, but he was aggrieved by the boldness and impudence of such people. How dare they, the Psalmist seems to be saying. By breaking God's Laws they are disavowing knowledge of God. And why does he say that? In verse 54 we read how God's Laws are his song. They are his delight and he holds them in his heart. They go with him wherever he travels and nobody can take them away from him.

Continuing in the same vein, those who actively obey God, putting into practise His commands, remember God perpetually. God works when His people listen to Him and acknowledge Him for who He is. The Psalmist sets himself up against those who mock him, and because they mock him are therefore despising God. He invites all others to stand up to those who slander God, whether that despising slander is active or passive. The Psalmist seeks a life of total obedience to God alone – both in the day and in the night. He immerses himself in God's word all day and thinks about it as he goes to sleep. Now remember, for the Psalmist the only part of the bible he would have had would be the first 5 books and possibly the book of Job. So he only has those stories of how God has encountered and interacted with people to reflect on and remember yet he still has a level of confidence in God that would probably put most of us to shame.

How are you doing when people mock and scorn you for your beliefs? How do you react when you see God being mocked, scorned and insulted? Are you living only for what you deem to be Godly experiences or are you living for God alone? Where the Psalmist probably only had 6 books talking about God encountering people, we have 66 books.

Not only that, we also have over 2,000 years of church history to see how God has used His people for His glory. That's the value of church history. Seeing how God has used people such as Athanasius, John Chrysostom, Augustine, Martin Luther, and John Calvin. Or more modern people such as Martin Luther King, Billy Graham or Mother Teresa. Nothing you are enduring or undergoing is new. Somebody, at some time, will have undergone a very similar experience, particularly in the Bible. Read the Bible and ask the Holy Spirit to help you learn and remember. Why? So that God will be actively obeyed in your life. Remember God and His word, so you can speak out against injustices in this world as you see them being reported in the media.

Are you getting to know your God personally as you read what it says? Do you pray with your Bible open? The role of memory is important to the Christian, even if you, like me, have memory problems. Be ready for the Holy Spirit to bring back to your memory the verses you read, when you need to remember them most – either when counselling other people or as help for yourself. The Psalmist remembered God's Word and saw its importance in the role of memorising Scripture. We would do well, to do likewise.

Stanza 8. Heth

(Dave Roberts)

[57] You are my portion, LORD;
I have promised to obey your words.
[58] I have sought your face with all my heart;
be gracious to me according to your promise.
[59] I have considered my ways
and have turned my steps to your statutes.
[60] I will hasten and not delay
to obey your commands.
[61] Though the wicked bind me with ropes,
I will not forget your law.
[62] At midnight I rise to give you thanks
for your righteous laws.
[63] I am a friend to all who fear you,
to all who follow your precepts.
[64] The earth is filled with your love, LORD;
teach me your decrees.

The Psalmist starts off this segment with a bang. A great burst of exclamation of praise "You are my portion Lord" Wow. Here he is lost in awe and wonder of the great God in whom he has put his trust and hope. This great God is who the Psalmist desires to obey and live wholeheartedly for with great devotion. This God is part of his treasure and he is totally and completely enraptured. You can tell that the Psalmist's heart is firmly set on the gift-giver, the Great God. So much so that he reaffirms yet again his promise to obey God's every law, precept and command.

Here is a man expressing total heartfelt devotion to the God who chose him and therefore seeks to serve Yahweh God. God may have chosen the Psalmist, but he still desires to develop the relationship with God. He seeks God's face fervently, wholeheartedly and with great devotion. By seeking God's face (verse 58), he is seeking to be in the very presence of the Living God, enfolded in the grace of God. At the very core of God's being are grace, love and mercy. And the Psalmist knows that God will give him grace, love and mercy, because God has promised that He will. And God always keeps his promises, his side of the deal.

As a response, in verses 59 & 60, the Psalmist considers how he has been living which may have been disobediently, at least in his judgement – though we might not have seen much wrong in the way he lived - and turns back to following and obeying the great God who is his portion, his all. That is repentance.

The Psalmist had stepped out of sync with God as we learn from the next stanza but turned himself around to the God of grace and made a conscious choice to obey God instead of going his own way. He chose the way of Life instead of the path leading to destruction. It is a lifelong commitment. The Psalmist is not making a half-hearted gesture. The Psalmist is taking all the steps he can in order to be found fully obedient to God and God's law. The Psalmist's enemies and persecutors may try to bind him with ropes and try to ensnare him, yet he will not forget God and God's words.

Nothing deflects him from following God; not being tied up by enemies who oppress and seek to restrict him, even kill him. The Psalmist knows they cannot match the God of grace whom he seeks. So when he had the opportunity, he arose at the midnight hour. Not in order to pray for deliverance but to give thanks. Give thanks, not that he may suffer for the sake of his God, but more to thank the Lord for His righteous laws. God's judgement will fall upon the wicked, the disobedient and unruly.

The Psalmist was a friend with those who feared the Lord. This is not fear as we think of fear. It is awe, respect, honouring the Lord as who he is fully and unreservedly. So this is about those who chose to obey God. These were the truly wise people, because the fear of the Lord, in this sense, is the beginning of wisdom. It didn't matter whether they were rich or poor – if they feared the Lord and obeyed Him, the Psalmist would be with them and befriend them. The Psalmist befriending the obscure who feared the Lord they served together.

Whatever the Psalmist had faced in his life, and there are hints here, and elsewhere in the Psalm that he had a tough and dangerous life, he knew that God had been there and loved him. Through exile, betrayal, war, peace, famine and prosperity – God has always shown His love to the Psalmist. This assures him that the Lord truly is his portion. He is so much in love with God he constantly seeks to be taught by Him. "Lord you are my portion", he said as he started this stanza and he finishes with another exclamation of how the earth is filled with the love of the Lord

How are you doing when faced with the problems of daily living? Where do you place the great God in your everyday concerns?   He desires most earnestly to be your full portion for every day. He calls you to seek His face. God the Holy Spirit indwells you, empowers you, transforms you and teaches you how to live. You are to be constantly filled with the Spirit, not just as a one off experience or an occasional experience in times of excitement.

The main way to accomplish this is through the Bible. Read it, pray it and be eager to learn from it. Don't be distracted by anything but be found fully seeking God in all facets and aspects of life. When times of trouble come, you will find that the Bible and the Holy Spirit's inspiration will help you, give you succour and comfort, as the gracious God of mercy enfolds you in His loving arms of compassion.

Seek Him. Desire to live rightly for Him. Show others you know Him, by doing good deeds and showing this God of love to those around you who do not fear Him. Build friendships with those you know who love the Lord as you do - regardless of their social status or rank. May you be discovered exclaiming that the Lord is your portion also.

Stanza 9. Teth

(Dave Roberts)

⁶⁵ Do good to your servant
according to your word, LORD.
⁶⁶ Teach me knowledge and good judgment,
for I trust your commands.
⁶⁷ Before I was afflicted I went astray,
but now I obey your word.
⁶⁸ You are good, and what you do is good;
teach me your decrees.
⁶⁹ Though the arrogant have smeared me with lies,
I keep your precepts with all my heart.
⁷⁰ Their hearts are callous and unfeeling,
but I delight in your law.
⁷¹ It was good for me to be afflicted
so that I might learn your decrees.
⁷² The law from your mouth is more precious to me
than thousands of pieces of silver and gold.

Just like in the previous section, the Psalmist starts again with a great acclamation. "Oh my Lord God. You have done good to your servant, according to your word". It is a statement of confidence from the Psalmist that the Lord will only do good to and for him. Here he acclaims God for his faithfulness and for the consistency of God's innate goodness. God has kept his promises to His servant, the Psalmist, and is faithful to him - and always will be.

From God's promises, flow the benefits of serving the Living God. Then the servant, the Psalmist, asks the Great God to teach him knowledge and judgment, for without either he could not live rightly in accordance with God's commandments and precepts. This is a man willing to be a servant of the Lord, with a teachable mind and a malleable spirit even, probably, in the difficulties of an oriental court with plenty of backstabbing, hopefully metaphorical, going on. So by the renewing of his mind and the gain of knowledge, he seeks to use this knowledge wisely and in good taste and judgement as he makes decisions.

But from verse 67 we see that The Psalmist had not always done so. He had gone astray from being obedient to God. Whether it was one incident or if he is relating himself to the natural rebelliousness against

God that all people have we do not know. He now seeks to be fully obedient to God, in mind, heart and in service. His zealousness for God and God's law is palpable. You can taste it as you read how he went from rebellion to obedience and submission to God's ways and laws.

Whatever the Psalmist's affliction was, it certainly had a curative effect on him. As he looked back on his life, the Psalmist saw what God had done and how God had brought him through, teaching him and loving him. The Psalmist could see that rebellion and insolence marked the historical Israel's relationship with God and how God had repeatedly tried to teach and mould them, but they had rejected his effort with the self-will that the Lord himself had given them.

Verse 68 sees the servant, the Psalmist, yet again pleading, begging and beseeching God to teach him. Teach me your decrees O great God. O Great God you are good and goodness is you. All that God does is good, the Psalmist cries, because goodness is part of the innate and essential character of God. He knows that God is good and good all the time. But knowing God is good, the Psalmist doesn't seek or pray for wealth, honours or privilege. By no means. The Psalmist seeks and prays continually to be taught how to obey this great and awesome God who is worthy of being fully obeyed.

The Psalmist then compares his antagonists with God. His proud enemies have worked against him. Does The Psalmist now wish to take revenge upon them? No. The Psalmist desires once again with heartfelt yearning to learn from God and keep his precepts and statutes in his heart. These opponents of his have hearts of impenetrable and unmovable stone. They have no feelings or sensitivity to the ways of God.

All this could well discourage the Psalmist; leaving him depressed, feeling defeated, battered, bruised and beaten. But again, no. The Spirit of God pierces the Psalmist's heart and he is shown to be malleable and teachable. The Psalmist is willing to be obedient to this God he serves. The Psalmist's delight is not in seeking revenge, but in reading about God and his innate goodness and Law.

This is one of the places where we see how the Psalmist did not look at the written words of God and think that was all. No, he regards them as the starting off point from which he will be able to interact with God, be taught, learn, grow develop in his faith. During his affliction, The Psalmist may well have questioned God, and asked "Why me?" He may well have been feeling quite dissolute during these times. But now, after the event, he says that it was good because God chastised him. That was part of God's method of teaching him, because God loved him. The Psalmist knew that he was naturally obstinate and opposed against God. He now knew that obedience is better than sacrifice and that what God wanted from him, was his utter and total obedience.

No amount of sacrifice could beat that. In this last verse, The Psalmist again states that his primary desire is not for honour or riches but rather to listen to God speaking to him through the Word. That is awesome isn't it? God is good and good all the time. Good in who He is. Good in what He does. Good in what He does to teach us.

Our response, as it was for the Psalmist, should be total obedience to this God of goodness. Yet, if we are honest, we have to say at least to ourselves, that sometimes we don't feel or see this goodness of God. We are all naturally rebellious and disobedient against God. God demands our obedience and conformity to Him.

Not as a means to salvation, because that could only ever be by His grace and mercy. We show we are His people, by being obedient to Him – which consists of loving Him and loving others. We are also to love getting to know Him, and have zealousness for the Bible and for prayer. Read about how God is good in your Bible and pray to Him to teach you. He will. We are to be obedient by serving others and if we do this reveals that we are serving this Almighty God of goodness. Then we too, like the Psalmist, will be servant hearted, teachable, humble and obedient, shining as lights in darkness.

Stanza 10. Yodh

(Jim Harris)

[73] Your hands made me and formed me;
give me understanding to learn your commands.
[74] May those who fear you rejoice when they see me,
for I have put my hope in your word.
[75] I know, LORD, that your laws are righteous,
and that in faithfulness you have afflicted me.
[76] May your unfailing love be my comfort,
according to your promise to your servant.
[77] Let your compassion come to me that I may live,
for your law is my delight.
[78] May the arrogant be put to shame for wronging me
without cause;
but I will meditate on your precepts.
[79] May those who fear you turn to me,
those who understand your statutes.
[80] May I wholeheartedly follow your decrees,
that I may not be put to shame.

When writing this psalm in honour of God's word and its effect upon the life of a believer, the author majored on 8 Hebrew words to describe ways in which the Lord communicates with his people as we saw in the introduction to these studies. All 8 are to be found in this section. Now what does that say to us? This section is about the powerful effect the word of God has in shaping us, developing us, maturing us and equipping us to represent Him in this world. Four big ideas came out of it for me.

Verses 73 and 80 remind us that God made us. 'Your hands made me and formed me.' That's the starting point for everyone who has a living relationship with God through the Lord Jesus Christ. We are not here by accident, nor by the will and activity of our parents alone. God was in the process of bringing us into the world. He is our Creator, so who knows better than He does how we work and what we need to know, so that we can live in His way?

Every piece of equipment in our homes was designed and built for a specific purpose. To know how to use it properly you read the manufacturer's instructions. If it needs servicing or repair you find information in that maker's manual – the Bible. It's ordinary common sense. It is also spiritual common sense to know that the best way to live in line with the Lord's purpose in making us, is to read his word and respond to its directions.

Verses 74 and 79 imply that the life of a true believer, especially someone active in the Lord's work, is bound to influence other people. You can't escape it. People around us will be affected, for better or worse, by the way we live (or don't live) in accordance with Scripture. Younger and less mature Christians look to those who are more experienced, for guidance and example. Others will be taking note of our words and actions and won't hesitate to charge us with any inconsistency they see in our behaviour.

This is true within the fellowship of a church, as well as in the home and at work. Our actions speak louder than our words, so we must let the Holy Spirit teach us through Scripture and keep in step with him in our lives. The New Testament has a lot to say about the importance of being a good witness before other people. 'Let your light shine before others, that they may see your good deeds and glorify your Father in heaven.' Matthew 5:16.

Verses 75 and 78 show that the Psalmist had to suffer for his faith. The life and work he was called to were no easy ride. He speaks of 'the arrogant' and the fact that he'd been wronged by these very people. Under the surface of the text, there is a suggestion that they'd misrepresented him; twisted his words and actions to suit their own ends. That's not easy to bear.

Paul wrote, in 2 Timothy 3:12, "In fact, everyone who wants to live a godly life in Christ Jesus will be persecuted,' It is not optional. But our Psalmist recognises that God is at work in all this, using it to knock him into shape. He bravely goes so far as to state in verse 75 'In faithfulness you have afflicted me.' No-one volunteers for suffering but we endure when it comes, for 'The testing of your faith develops perseverance.' (James 1:3)

Finally, we notice 5 'wish prayers'; short prayers beginning with the word 'May ...' Pick them out and think about them. These are not weak prayers. They are valid and honest, reaching from the heart into other people's lives and needs. They may be expressed at any time, in any place, for anyone. Simple, but real. The apostle Paul used 'wish prayers'. Look up Romans 15:5-6, 13, for two examples. Sometimes, when we find normal prayer difficult, these short prayers can prove valuable in helping us dispense a blessing on other people. Why not try to find ways of using this kind of prayer as an add-on to your usual methods of praying?

Stanza 11. Kaph

(Dave Roberts)

[81] My soul faints with longing for your salvation,
but I have put my hope in your word.
[82] My eyes fail, looking for your promise;
I say, "When will you comfort me?"
[83] Though I am like a wineskin in the smoke,
I do not forget your decrees.
[84] How long must your servant wait?
When will you punish my persecutors?
[85] The arrogant dig pits to trap me,
contrary to your law.
[86] All your commands are trustworthy;
help me, for I am being persecuted without cause.
[87] They almost wiped me from the earth,
but I have not forsaken your precepts.
[88] In your unfailing love preserve my life,
that I may obey the statutes of your mouth.

The Psalmist knows that salvation will come to him, because God has promised it and God always keeps His promises. The Psalmist knows God will rescue him because God never disappoints. When desire is exhausted and extinguished, then a certain and sure hope takes over to lift the Psalmist back up again. With weakened eyes the Psalmist seeks comfort and ease.

The picture of wineskins being smoked is the most striking metaphor in all this long poem but perhaps strange to us in the twenty first century world. But for The Psalmist they were an explicit illustration of his condition. Wineskins when empty were hung up in the tent and when smoke filled the tent as it often did, the wineskins grew haggard, wrinkled from the heat and blackened with soot.

It's a picture of The Psalmist's face. He feels decrepit, wrinkled, haggard and gloomy. His body is feeling listless and dilapidated. He had endured persecution, undergone the torment of slanderous lies being told about him and his character has been blackened as if with soot.

And yet... and yet he still had hope, a glimmer of anticipation – he does not forget God's decrees and statutes. This is his way of reaching out to hold God's hand through this time. He is waiting for his God to deliver & rescue him, to realise the hope he had placed in Yahweh God. The Psalmist was getting edgy and fed up. He has placed his grievances against others into the court of the Lord and was waiting for justice to be done.

He wants his persecutors punished according to God's law. His persecutors were digging him many pits in which to trap and bury him. They were contravening God's law with jesting, arrogance and a haughty step. But the Psalmist's enemies had forgotten that while they were his enemies, because he was one of the Lord's people they were also enemies of God.

God who had decreed and given commandments to be followed which they were now breaking. The Psalmist had followed God's commands so he would be rescued from his tormentors perhaps not immediately, but eventually. The Psalmist had not forgotten about God and His promises. God will help him and the Psalmist is stretching out his hands for help.

And isn't this last verse more than delightful. It is not only the Psalmist saying spare or preserve my life. We get a sense it is more a case of "Give me life." The Psalmist is not seeking merely survival but wanting a full life restored to him. And he knows that this God he follows and serves will grant him new life. The Psalmist will live again. God has promised it. It is as if the Psalmist is saying "I want to be born again!" WOW.

Despite what he is going through, The Psalmist knows he will have new life. This new life will see The Psalmist continue to exhibit a life worthy of God as he follows God's commands in a dynamic relationship. What God has said, The Psalmist will do. The Psalmist was assuredly a man after God's own heart.

How are you doing right now? Are you feeling as the Psalmist was? Confused, aged, and drying up, wrinkled and lacking energy – physically and/or spiritually? Are people mocking you and jeering at you because of the faith you have in Jesus Christ? Take heart, for God is watching, protecting and will rescue you. Stay faithful to Him despite all the opposition you are enduring and the Great God whom you seek to serve will come to your aid. Don't give in to the doubters by compromising yourself but hold true to God and His word.

If you are the subject of abuse, injustice, undue pressure at work or in the family, or any kind of wrongdoing, take your case to God in prayer. Let the God of justice help you, give you counsel through the

Bible and minister to you. Ask the Holy Spirit to give you comfort, for that is one of his names – the Comforter. Whatever you are going through reach out and touch God's hand that is outstretched to you. Reach out in gratitude to the great God and as an act of gratitude, seek to live a holy life worthy of being called His servant.

Stanza 12. Lamedh

(Dave Roberts)

[89] Your word, LORD, is eternal;
it stands firm in the heavens.
[90] Your faithfulness continues through all generations;
you established the earth, and it endures.
[91] Your laws endure to this day,
for all things serve you.
[92] If your law had not been my delight,
I would have perished in my affliction.
[93] I will never forget your precepts,
for by them you have preserved my life.
[94] Save me, for I am yours;
I have sought out your precepts.
[95] The wicked are waiting to destroy me,
but I will ponder your statutes.
[96] To all perfection I see a limit;
but your commands are boundless.

From languishing in the pit of despair in the previous section, the Psalmist here starts with a bang – "Your word, O Lord, is eternal, it stands firm in the heavens". While in the pit, he was being tossed and turned like a small boat on a stormy sea. Now he has focussed on a steady rock – God's word. It is ordered, steadfast, secure and timeless. In his times of trouble, he turns his attention from himself and his troubles to something much more certain – the Lord and his word, Law, precepts, commands, promises, decrees, laws and statutes. God's promises are so certain, assured, and secure that the Psalmist places his whole hope in them. Secure in the Psalmist's mind and heart is the knowledge that God will rescue him as promised and God is a God of faithfulness.

He goes on in the next verse to continue the WOW factor. The Psalmist knows that God's faithfulness is unchangeable, timeless and persevering. Look here at the correlation between God's word and God's work. Just as He is faithful throughout time to all generations, so He created the whole world at a single command, and it too endures. Just as the earth endures having been established by God's powerful Word, so too do God's laws endure with precision. God's word sustains all of creation and all things made are to serve Him, almighty God.

For the Psalmist this means that to serve God we have to obey God and live a life of service to God. The Psalmist learns to obey, by studying the instructions of God and the way these have worked out for his ancestors and ancient Israel. This same Word preserves the Psalmist. It is his utter delight. It is his succour, help and source of joy. Cogitating upon and remembering God's law is his way of being sustained. For without it, the Psalmist would be dust at the bottom of the pit – extinguished, lifeless, maligned and afflicted.

The Psalmist, lifts his mind to heaven and knows that the word of God stands secure there because heaven is as consistent and constant as what he can see – the earth that God established and maintains. There is his only hope, and that hope was found in God alone through God's word because, unlike him, God is not perishable. He reflects on how God's truths, precepts and instructions have been a source of comfort, joy and encouragement to him to keep going. Without them, he would have just given up and let his persecutors malign him further and even destroy him.

Because of this hope, the Psalmist reaches out to God to save him, because he knows that only God can rescue him. He reaches out to God through God's own precepts, law and word. The Psalmist's salvation can only come from God and so he acknowledges that God is his only hope as he discovered by reading through God's teachings and thus gaining knowledge of how God handled the Psalmist's ancestors.

While his persecutors wait for him, laying traps to ensnare and take his life, the Psalmist is taking comfort through what he knows about God through the word. He ponders the words of God, recalls them, brings to mind the promises made by God and the righteous laws given so that he can live a right life for God. The Psalmist doesn't worry what mere humans can do to him. No. He gets stuck in to getting to know God better and strengthening his relationship with God. That is what matters to him – being close to God, studying God and becoming closer to God through pondering God's word and God's decrees.

Then finally, the Psalmist concludes that all is meaningless and limited apart from God and God's utterances. God's commandments and laws bring freedom and hope. While all things visible have a degree of perfection, they are also temporary, unstable and narrow. Through the trials of life, the only hope that sustained him was God's ways and God's word. Its perfection is its glory. By acknowledging that he falls far short of God's holiness and glory, he continues in the knowledge that his salvation can only come from God. It is not his perfection he seeks as a means to being rescued, but God's perfection. It is not by using his own strength but God's strength to save.

How are you doing and what do you do when the trials of life hit you with a bang? Do you go into your shell and take pity on yourself? Do you think God doesn't care about you and your situation? It's all very well saying you are on God's side when things are going well, but life here on earth just isn't like that all the time. That is not reality. Reality is what God wants to help you with. He has promised to help you; promised to sustain you and promised to be in relationship with you. Are you worrying and burdened? Then tell God about it, and cast your burdens upon Jesus and let him take the load.

Are you serving God and God's people and yet feeling weak? Pray and ask God to empower you with the Holy Spirit, so that you do things using His inexhaustible energy and indefatigable power. Where does your help come from? It comes from God and from pondering what He has said in the Bible, helping to build your relationship with Him.

Stanza 13. Mem

(Dave Roberts)

[97] Oh, how I love your law.
I meditate on it all day long.
[98] Your commands are always with me
and make me wiser than my enemies.
[99] I have more insight than all my teachers,
for I meditate on your statutes.
[100] I have more understanding than the elders,
for I obey your precepts.
[101] I have kept my feet from every evil path
so that I might obey your word.
[102] I have not departed from your laws,
for you yourself have taught me.
[103] How sweet are your words to my taste,
sweeter than honey to my mouth.
[104] I gain understanding from your precepts;
therefore I hate every wrong path.

Here the Psalmist declares his love for God's commands, law and wisdom. It's now not merely delight but he has moved on to a kind of spiritual ecstatic love. So much so, that the Psalmist meditates on God's law all the time, letting what God has revealed in His written word permeate his whole thinking. Of course, meditating in this sense is not just sitting around and thinking – meditating in the biblical sense is always focussed on God and then acting out what has been learnt from God.

The Psalmist knows that action has its beginning in the thought process and is the culmination of meditating. This action makes the Psalmist wiser than his enemies. (In fact what he says gives a bad impression of his enemies, teachers and elders.) Because he relies on the words of God and obeys what God has said, the Psalmist can avoid the traps of his enemies. He knows that God will protect him. He is endeavouring to live a life worth of His God – a life of total obedience and worship. By having God's commands with him all the time, he has every chance of achieving this twin aim. And it's not only his enemies that he is wiser than – it is also his teachers.

It's not that these teachers were fools – they were not. They were clearly operating in ways that were not based on the Word of God but on human ideas. It is the study of God's word and meditating upon it that leads to wisdom and fear of the Lord. He doesn't just accept what those around him and teach him say. He tests and approves their teaching in comparison with what he finds in the Law.

Think not that the Psalmist is boasting, because he is not. Rather, he is accepting the teaching from God's word with a child-like desire to grow in knowledge and obedience of Almighty God. He builds up God and God's Law and not himself. This has also led him to be more obedient than his elders. God's precepts and commandments are a priority in the life of the Psalmist. He exudes ecstatic love for God and for God's law, precepts, statutes and commandments. And this ecstatic desire has produced dividends. The Psalmist's feet have been on the path of obedience and right living. He is following God intimately. Every footstep he takes is carefully chosen so that his feet stay away from the paths of evil. Nothing could persuade or seduce him away from following God's path closely.

So intimate is he with God's commandments and statutes that he has not departed from them. The path of obedience to God may not have been the easiest path for the Psalmist to take, but it was the right path because it showed obedience to Almighty God, the greatest teacher of all (v102). This intimacy of relationship between the Psalmist and God is beautifully sweet and dynamic. The Psalmist loves to read the words of God and exclaims that it is even sweeter when he speaks the words of God.

While God's commands are to be sweet to the ears, eyes and intellect, it is surpassed in sweetness when talked about and put into action. The Psalmist knew that if he only gained head knowledge of obedience to God, then he would stray away from God, so he puts into practice in his life what God has taught him to do. He has to live a life of total and utter obedience to the great God he worships and adores. Try as they might, his enemies cannot seduce him away from this obedience to his God.

This life of total obedience to God was mirrored in the life of Jesus Christ. Many times he was tempted to give in, walk the easy path and live a life unworthy of God. While we know the Psalmist did sin, we know for sure that Jesus Christ did not. The life of Jesus Christ portrays an unparalleled intimacy with God and an ecstatic desire to be obedient to God. Jesus could have said 'no' to the cross, but he did not. When Jesus Christ died on that cross, it was part of His total obedience to

God. The Apostle Matthew records Jesus enduring temptations by satan in Matthew 4:1-11. Jesus could have given into satan's temptations but we know that He did not. He had faith that His Father would raise him to life again 3 days later (Matthew 27:63) – and He did. Jesus had intimate knowledge of the Scriptures and of the Lord as did the Psalmist.

How are you doing? Are there areas in your life where you are not obeying God and are being seduced away from Him? How is your intimacy with Him? Do you have an ecstatic relationship with the Bible, God's written word, as the Psalmist did? Why not pray and ask the Holy Spirit to develop this spiritual ecstasy within you, to read the Bible and follow it closely. So we wrap up with wise words from the Apostle Paul, writing in Ephesians 5:15-16 "Be very careful, then, how you live – not as unwise but as wise, making the most of every opportunity, because the days are evil.

Stanza 14. Nun

(Dave Roberts)

[105] Your word is a lamp for my feet,
a light on my path.
[106] I have taken an oath and confirmed it,
that I will follow your righteous laws.
[107] I have suffered much;
preserve my life, LORD, according to your word.
[108] Accept, LORD, the willing praise of my mouth,
and teach me your laws.
[109] Though I constantly take my life in my hands,
I will not forget your law.
[110] The wicked have set a snare for me,
but I have not strayed from your precepts.
[111] Your statutes are my heritage forever;
they are the joy of my heart.
[112] My heart is set on keeping your decrees
to the very end.

If the last section was about Spiritual ecstasy, then this one is about Spiritual joy, and we will aim to see what it is that brings the Psalmist spiritual joy. As he walks in the darkness, with a lamp to show him where to tread and which path to follow, the Psalmist here is reflecting on just how God's word leads, guides and keeps him on the path of staying right with, and obedient to, Almighty God.

Now, he says just how brightly shining God's word is, to guide, steer and keep him on the narrow spiritual path. The light of Scripture and God's Law, commands and statues not only gives guidance on how to live, but also directs and guides every action. God's word, says the Psalmist, is a light and lamp through the dark time he spoke of earlier. The tiniest light affects even the darkest night. He recognizes that it is after having renounced all earthly wisdom that he will be guided by heavenly wisdom seen in the Law. With a lamp to direct his footsteps and a light to guide his path, the Psalmist resolved boldly before God, that he would follow the righteous laws as laid down.

The lamp and the light are to show God's moral guidance. They are to show a way forward and not backwards. If he goes backwards, the Psalmist knows he will fall into darkness and ways that are disobedient to God. So he relies on the Law and God's commandments to show him the way up the narrow path of obedience to God. He offers himself to the service of God and is willing to fully commit to following where God leads and be obedient to Him.

With his desire to keep God's laws, the Psalmist is embracing what God commands wholeheartedly and single-mindedly. And how does he achieve this? Is this achievable by using his own strength and guile? No. It's only by God's grace and power that the Psalmist can hope to achieve his goal and fulfil his oath. He knows that even though he suffers for his obedience, the Lord has promised to save and rescue him, according to His promises.

Again, the Psalmist relies on God's promises to save, secure and rescue him. In response to being rescued, the Psalmist offers praises and a willingness to be taught. Nothing was more important to the Psalmist than to know how God wanted him to behave in all situations and God's laws, statutes, precepts and commands enable the Psalmist to exercise Godly obedience in all situations – both private and public. He has sought to do this, despite sufferings, persecutions, having his very life threatened and being in constant danger from his enemies.

Despite all that, God's laws are imprinted on the Psalmist's heart and engraved on his mind he does not forget. He is then able to overcome the traps, lures, snares and temptations laid out in wait for him, by his enemies. Knowing God's precepts on his heart and mind, allow the Psalmist to avoid such traps, shining the lamp and light of God's word on the path ahead. His persecuting enemies seek to destroy and kill him, but they are defeated by the Psalmist's Godly guile and knowledge. For the Psalmist knows that God's laws are from everlasting to everlasting and they bring him true joy.

The testimonies he has read in the history of his people about how they overcame in order to be obedient to God are a joy to him. Provided the Psalmist possessed this everlasting joy, he could leave all other pleasures such as music, gold, jewels, riches, honours, wealth and family behind. God and being obedient to God through God's laws were the Psalmists utmost joy and goal – with a lamp and light to show the way forward.

How is your lamp showing? How is your walk of obedience to, and service of, God going? It is when we are struggling with temptations and sins that we need the Holy Spirit to help us overcome. So often, I know, we try in our own strength to overcome temptations and then we fail. We succumb to the tempter's traps and disobey God much to the pleasure of our goading enemies. Jesus in the last night before his arrest, trial and death, endured supreme temptations to just give up. But He didn't, because like the Psalmist, His supreme joy was found in obedience to the Father. Then again we are not always under great pressure. And those times are just as dangerous. Apathy can set in and we become cool towards the Lord without really realising what is happening. In these times as well we need to make sure that we keep our feet on the right path. It is so easy to lie down beside the undemanding path and go to sleep.

But we too have taken an oath and confirmed it. We too have a duty to follow through thick and thin. Where is your supreme joy found? Is it found in your wealth, possessions, sexual activity, friends or family? Or is your supreme joy, like the Psalmist and Jesus, found in obedience to God and service to Him and His people? Remember that we have a helper who dwells inside us – God the Holy Spirit. He will help you through temptations and snares and freely give you the grace to do so.

Finally, when you do sin, having fallen for the lure

or trap of the enemy, then be quick to ask forgiveness for your sin. The longer you leave it, the more it will fester, turns poisonous and gives the enemy, satan, an opportunity to accuse you. Ask forgiveness from God, accept His grace, move on and ask the Holy Spirit to fill you anew and help you. Read Psalm 51 and Psalm 32 if you want to know how David did it.

Stanza 15. Samekh

(Dave Roberts)

[113] I hate double-minded people,

but I love your law.

[114] You are my refuge and my shield;

I have put my hope in your word.

[115] Away from me, you evildoers,

that I may keep the commands of my God.

[116] Sustain me, my God, according to your promise,

and I shall live;

do not let my hopes be dashed.

[117] Uphold me, and I shall be delivered;

I shall always have regard for your decrees.

[118] You reject all who stray from your decrees,

for their delusions come to nothing.

[119] All the wicked of the earth you discard like dross;

therefore I love your statutes.

[120] My flesh trembles in fear of you;

I stand in awe of your laws.

Just as he is single-minded regarding God, obeying God and keeping God's law, so there are others who are unstable and are in two minds about how to act. The Psalmist compares the stability and reliability of God's word with the instability and fluctuations of those who are unstable in their commitment to God and God alone. Even his own thoughts when he strays, are the product of a mind that is having wayward thoughts.

The Psalmist knows that only God's word and God's wisdom can provide a solid basis for making decisions, whether moral, private or public. We get the sense that he is fighting a battle within himself, to control his thoughts and thinking patterns – that, when his old ways of thinking habitually take over, he hates it. He goes on to cry out to God that God alone is his rescuer, refuge and protector. He cannot rely on his own intellect and man-made wisdom to do that for him, but rather, he relies on God's word and God's wisdom to reveal God as his protector and shelter.

Then in verse 115, we see that he has a battle not only within himself, but also with those who would seek to harm him. These people are taunting him, tempting him and seeking to destroy him. Perhaps they are mocking him for his belief in God's words and wisdom, which is why he reacts by saying he wants to keep the commandments of his protecting God. With God at his side, the Psalmist knows that either no harm will come to him or if it does the Lord will be with him through his problems.

He has a personal relationship with this God and he wants to follow him closely. The taunts of his enemies are as nothing. The Psalmist takes refuge in the wisdom of His All-knowing God. His God has promised to sustain him and maintain his life. The Psalmist has put all his hopes in and on this great God whom he desires to know more and more. He knows God's promises are true, unlike those made by his enemies. God will not forsake him, even when all other people do. When he is in trouble, to whom does he turn? Does he turn to his enemies and surrender? Does he rely on his own wisdom and guile to escape the clutches of those who would do him harm?

No! The Psalmist knows that God Himself will deliver him from the clutches of evil, and that by paying regard to God's decrees and God's wisdom, he will escape. He doesn't want to obey mere man but rather be obedient to this great God whom he loves, cherishes, adores and who has promised to deliver him from evil and those who do evil. God Himself will reject those who reject God and God's ways.

They are living a life of deceit, double-mindedness and fluctuating morals – God will reject them because they have paid Him no heed. They have relied on their own wisdom and guile to survive – but not for much longer. The Psalmist knows that this God rules the earth and all those who do wicked things and are not in relationship with Him, will be lost forever.

The Psalmist knows that it is by his God's twin actions of mercy and grace that he will be delivered and because he loves this God, he also loves all that God has commanded him to do. He is in fear of this awesome, all-powerful God and is in awe of the wisdom given in the laws and commands of this God. Those that rely on their own wisdom, own imagination, own power will be as dust in the wind – but those that fear the Lord, accept His wisdom and commands, will be delivered, rescued and be alive forever - just as the Psalmist says.

I don't know about you, but I face a constant battle to be obedient to God and His wisdom. When we are tempted to sin, we are given two choices – either to sin or not to sin. We hop from one leg to the other, not knowing which leg to stand on. By continuing to ponder the temptation, we fall into a double-minded state. We can choose to either obey God or disobey Him. Three enemies surround us: satan, the world and our old nature. We are to be over-comers of these enemies and not in our own strength, wisdom or guile. If we put our trust in anybody or anything but God the Holy Spirit to help us overcome the temptation to sin, we will fall into that trap of double-mindedness that the Psalmist talks about. We too will then be jumping from one leg to the other, not knowing how to stand.

We can overcome our enemies and temptations by asking God the Holy Spirit to help us escape the trap and by also having a reverent fear of God. Fear – awe, honour, trustful dependence - of the Lord is the beginning of wisdom cries the writer of Proverbs. It is a fear borne out of respect rather than dread. It is a fear borne from being in total awe.

So let's go ever onwards, not hopping from one leg to the other or from one thought to another, but rather getting to know God's word intimately, being stable in our thinking and in our fearful desire to please this awesome God of grace and mercy, who delivers, rescues, protects and shelters. And it is in this God, that I take rest in my new nature given to me when I became a Christian and letting Him fight the battles for me. So, I hope, do you.

Stanza 16. Ayin

(Jim Harris)

¹²¹ I have done what is righteous and just;
do not leave me to my oppressors.
¹²² Ensure your servant's well-being;
do not let the arrogant oppress me.
¹²³ My eyes fail, looking for your salvation,
looking for your righteous promise.
¹²⁴ Deal with your servant according to your love
and teach me your decrees.
¹²⁵ I am your servant; give me discernment
that I may understand your statutes.
¹²⁶ It is time for you to act, LORD;
your law is being broken.
¹²⁷ Because I love your commands
more than gold, more than pure gold,
¹²⁸ and because I consider all your precepts right,
I hate every wrong path.

Three times in these eight verses you'll find the words 'your servant'. That gives a flavour to this section of the psalm. The Psalmist knows that he has been called in his personal life and, probably, in a public role to serve the Lord. He feels the cost of doing that and appeals to the Lord for help in various ways.

All true believers in Jesus today are called to serve the Lord. It begins with simply the way we live. That means that our lifestyle, our priorities and our values about what is right and wrong, will often bring us into conflict with people living and working around us. Should the Lord call us into a specific role in serving Him, in our local church perhaps, or in the wider world through a Christian mission or agency, the pressure will come in a different way, from those who object to the work we are doing in the name of Christ. Like the Psalmist we, too, must turn to the Lord for his comfort and strengthening in the situation.

In the first two verses here, the Psalmist is concerned for his own well-being. 'I have done what is righteous and just; do not leave me to my oppressors. Ensure your servant's well-being; do not let the arrogant oppress me.' He is suffering from 'people-pressure' and he's not too keen on it. But we take note of the fact that he's not engaging with them in a war of words but, rather, he's turned to the Lord with an urgent plea for His help. He's resorted to prayer, rather than to disputation, as the best way of dealing with the problem. That's a good example to follow.

Our arguments will tend to harden people in their opposition. Sometimes it will even give them some satisfaction to know that they've got to us. Like Jesus before his enemies, we will find that being silent before them but verbal towards God is usually the best way of handling the matter. After all, the Spirit of God can reach those parts in people that none of us can get to.It's clear that the Psalmist is being called to endure, to keep going, while the Lord is actually handling the situation for him. God's timing and the servant's wishes do not coincide. The Lord seems to be hanging about – why doesn't He get on with it? 'My eyes fail, looking for your salvation.'

And, in verse 126, a wake-up call to the Lord, 'It is time for you to act, Lord.' His impatience, on the one hand, is due to his humanity. He's sharing with us the stress we all feel when our prayers are not being answered with the degree of urgency we feel the case merits. On the other hand, he has a genuine concern, which those who profess to be God's people are actually flouting & breaking His Law. Now, whatever happens, or doesn't happen to him personally, surely that situation needs to be addressed. So, in verses 127-128 we read, 'Because I love your commands more than gold, more than pure gold, and because I consider all your precepts right, I hate every wrong path.' That kind of love for the Lord and his word runs through the whole of this challenging psalm.

In fact, it will be found everywhere in Scripture. Devotion to the Lord is expressed by a desire to live His way and to please Him. Many years later, the Apostle Paul would write this to the Christians at Colossae so that you may live a life worthy of the Lord and please him in every way: bearing fruit in every good work, growing in the knowledge of God,' Colossians 1:10.

Before we leave this servant of the Lord, let's have a look at verse 124. 'Deal with your servant according to your love.' That's a confident request, rooted in his experience of what God is like. He knows that 'God is love', therefore all God's dealings with us spring from that love, are informed and shaped by that love, and are working towards the best possible end for us.

At present, it seems God is working along a strange route and to a different timetable, but in the end, all will be well. Remember these words from the Apostle Paul,

'For I am convinced that neither death nor life, neither angels nor demons, neither the present nor the future, nor any powers, neither height nor depth, nor anything else in all creation, will be able to separate us from the love of God that is in Christ Jesus our Lord.' (Romans 8:38-39)

Read Romans 5:1-8, and let the Holy Spirit bring home to your heart the tremendous truth of God's love at work in you and for you, even in the most difficult of circumstances.

Stanza 17. Pe

(Jim Harris)

¹²⁹ Your statutes are wonderful;

therefore I obey them.

¹³⁰ The unfolding of your words gives light;

it gives understanding to the simple.

¹³¹ I open my mouth and pant,

longing for your commands.

¹³² Turn to me and have mercy on me,

as you always do to those who love your name.

¹³³ Direct my footsteps according to your word;

let no sin rule over me.

¹³⁴ Redeem me from human oppression,

that I may obey your precepts.

¹³⁵ Make your face shine on your servant

and teach me your decrees.

¹³⁶ Streams of tears flow from my eyes,

for your law is not obeyed.

This section of Psalm 119 makes us consider the role of the word of God in bringing understanding to our minds, moral and spiritual direction to our lives, and heart satisfaction in our relationship with the Lord. To ease us into this, we look elsewhere in Scripture first. In the book of Numbers, we read of the Aaronic Blessing. As the High Priest of the people of Israel, Aaron was instructed to bless them in the Name of the Lord.

> 'The LORD bless you and keep you;
> the LORD make his face shine on you
> and be gracious to you;
> the LORD turn his face toward you
> and give you peace.' (Numbers 6:24-26)

It's my feeling that this priestly blessing was in the psalmist's mind when he wrote this stanza,. 'Turn to me and be gracious to me' (verse 132). Part of being gracious is acceptance, forgiveness and peace. Then, in verse 135, he says, 'Make your face shine upon your servant'. So, he is asking God to turn towards him, to be gracious to him, to make his face shine upon him? I'm sure you can see the connection between this Psalm and that blessing.

How is the Christian equivalent of that blessing

conferred upon us today? It's done by the Holy Spirit through the word of God, the words of Scripture. Many church services include or conclude with these very words of Scripture, spoken as a 'benediction' or 'announcement of blessing from the Lord' upon his people.

It also happens in our personal lives. As we read, believe, and respond to the wonderful words of God, we receive a rich blessing upon ourselves. The very first verse picks this up, 'Your statutes are wonderful; therefore I obey them.' The last verse takes a different but related line, 'Streams of tears flow from my eyes, for your law is not obeyed.' Here's a man who really does understand the way in which the Lord confers his blessing upon his believing people, and grieves that there are those who profess to belong to the Lord but refuse to obey his word. Let's make sure that isn't true of any of us.

Now let's see how God's word brings his blessing, as we explore these verses. It begins by bringing understanding. Verse 130, 'The unfolding of you words gives light; it gives understanding to the simple.' By 'simple' he is not describing those with what we would call 'learning difficulties', but those whose understanding has not yet matured enough for them to be fully aware of God's will and ways. Where there's a willingness to learn about spiritual matters, the word of God will bring what the psalmist calls 'light'. This is a process which combines insight and wisdom. We gain further insight into the Lord and his ways with humankind; into the realm of spiritual realities and experience; into the whole meaning of Jesus and his work of redemption; into what it means to live by the Spirit, and so on.

We also receive the gift of wisdom, which enables us to apply what we know through insight to our lives in this world. That way we can live to the praise and glory of God. Scripture also gives us direction. It shows us the right way to live, morally and spiritually. That affects our attitudes towards other people and our relationships with them. We live by the combination of the grace and truth that was evident in the Lord Jesus. God's word also helps us pick our way through the moral maze of life in the twenty first century – what to avoid and what to be involved with. Verse 133, 'Direct my footsteps according to your word; let no sin rule over me.'

Finally, Scripture also enables us to enjoy heart-satisfaction in our relationship with the Lord. In verse 131 he is 'longing for (the Lord's) commands' and describes himself 'panting' like a thirsty animal. In 134 he wishes to be free from the force of human opinions and pressure, so that he can respond fully to the Lord.

In verse 135 he is looking for a shining sense of God's presence, as he responds to what the Lord shows him in his word. This is the language of a truly devotional life. To see a New Testament example of how all this fits together, read Luke 24:13-35 when you can, and see how what's written there can be true for us, as we walk through life in close fellowship with our risen Lord Jesus. Take particular note of verse 32, 'They asked each other, 'Were not our hearts burning within us while he talked with us on the road and opened the Scriptures to us?''

Stanza 18. Tsadhe

(Jim Harris)

[137] You are righteous, LORD,

and your laws are right.

[138] The statutes you have laid down are righteous;

they are fully trustworthy.

[139] My zeal wears me out,

for my enemies ignore your words.

[140] Your promises have been thoroughly tested,

and your servant loves them.

[141] Though I am lowly and despised,

I do not forget your precepts.

[142] Your righteousness is everlasting

and your law is true.

[143] Trouble and distress have come upon me,

but your commands give me delight.

[144] Your statutes are always righteous;

give me understanding that I may live.

The very first word introduces the dominant theme in this stanza. It's about God and things being 'right' or 'righteous'. Cast your eyes over verses 137, 138, 142 and 144. Then, looking at them more closely, we get to see something like this.

Verse 137 proclaims that God is righteous. 'You are righteous, Lord. This may be understood in terms of God's relationship with his people. He keeps his promises. He provides for their needs. He is faithful in all his deeds and ways. He always does what is right, for God cannot deny himself; God cannot lie; God cannot break his word, once given.

Verse 138 has a high view of God's statutes – another word describing the detail of God's Law. 'The statutes you have laid down are righteous; they are fully trustworthy.' They flow from God, therefore they are as dependable and effective as God himself is. If God said it, then you can rely on it.

Verse 140 reads, 'Your promises have been thoroughly tested, and your servant loves them.' God is righteous. He's consistent. If that is true, then what flows from God is also righteous.' God gave his Law through Moses. The detailed laws within it were designed to shape the crowd of people who escaped from slavery in Egypt, into a coherent nation fit to live in the Promised Land, where they would show the rest of the world what the LORD was really like. At least, that was the intention, but it's working out fell short of God's wishes, because his people were not altogether co-operative.

Verse 142, he comes back to the Lord himself, commenting, 'Your righteousness is everlasting and your law is true.' It all starts with the Lord, filters down through his Law – his word for his People – which, in turn shapes them to demonstrate what kind of a God he is.

And, finally, in verse 144 suggests the permanence of what God has said. 'Your statutes are always righteous; give me understanding that I may live.' Most of what has occupied his thought in this Psalm was written well before he was born, some of it many centuries before, yet he sees it as still relevant to him, because it flows from the righteous God.

In an earlier stanza, verses 89-90, he has already written, 'Your word, Lord, is eternal; it stands firm in the heavens. Your faithfulness continues through all generations.' The Lord isn't fickle or capricious, saying one thing now and a totally different thing a little later.

You can build your life on God's word, just as Jesus spoke of the wise and foolish builders in Matthew 7. Wise people always build on the truth that the Lord Jesus brought to us. And he, as Hebrews 13:8 tells us, 'is the same yesterday and today and for ever.'

So, that is the thrust of this passage for those of us who have committed our lives to Christ and are listed among his people. We have the word of God to a much greater extent than the psalmist did, in that we have both Old and New Testaments. If we don't have an appetite to read and hear it, ask the Holy Spirit to make us hungry for it.

If our lives are being shaped mostly by influences drawn from this world in which we live, let's open ourselves up to the Lord through Scripture, and ask the Holy Spirit to use it to make us more like the Lord himself, to whom we owe everything spiritually. If our reading of life's negative experiences causes us to doubt the goodness and love of God, let's soak our minds in the glorious truth of a passage like Romans 8 or the Gospel accounts of Jesus death and resurrection.

Stanza 19. Qoph

(Dave Roberts)

¹⁴⁵ I call with all my heart; answer me, LORD,
and I will obey your decrees.
¹⁴⁶ I call out to you; save me
and I will keep your statutes.
¹⁴⁷ I rise before dawn and cry for help;
I have put my hope in your word.
¹⁴⁸ My eyes stay open through the watches of the night,
that I may meditate on your promises.
¹⁴⁹ Hear my voice in accordance with your love;
preserve my life, LORD, according to your laws.
¹⁵⁰ Those who devise wicked schemes are near,
but they are far from your law.
¹⁵¹ Yet you are near, LORD,
and all your commands are true.
¹⁵² Long ago I learned from your statutes
that you established them to last for ever.

Here the Psalmist starts this section with two impassioned calls or loud cries. These are not necessarily loud audible cries but rather the inner desires of the heart and a bending of the will calling out to God. The first time is for God to hear him. His whole being – body, mind and soul –is crying out to God, pleading with Him with full mental, emotional and spiritual energy. These are impassioned pleas. The Psalmist is determinately anxious that God should hear him so he is promising obedience if only he can hear a word from the Lord. He is determined to live a life that is pleasing to God. To live a life that is worthy of being one who is called God's servant.

The Psalmist promises to follow God's instructions and statutes in full obedience. The Psalmist mentions that he has cried, pleaded, begged passionately for God to be with him. The Psalmist's prayers are frequent, intense and strong. So strong are his desires that the moment he wakes, he is in prayer and he gets up early so that he has time to pray before the busy–ness of the day starts.

A key element of his prayers is hope. Here he has put his hope in God and God's word. God is faithful, as the Psalmist has said throughout, and God's words are true – they can be relied upon to encourage and give hope. So intense is his prayer life, that not only is he up early in the morning to pray, but late at night he can be found to be meditating on the promises that God has made.

The Psalmist's prayers were all day long. From before dawn till after dusk. He prayed to and worshipped His God all day with great fervour and eagerness. He knows God will hear his voice, his pleadings as he maintains an attitude of hope, worship and adoration. And to reaffirm that, he knows that God is a great God of love and a God of great love.

Here in verse 149, it's an audible prayer, not through any merit of his own, but of the merits of God. This God is loving, kind and a great preserver. This God fulfils the promises He makes. He gives strength in order to overcome the burdens faced by the Psalmist. When the Psalmist is faced with death, the God he serves, gives more life. WOW.

The Psalmist doesn't concentrate on himself and what he says, but rather on this God and particularly His voice as seen in the laws. What he says and has said, particularly in his law. He will be rescued before his enemies can kill him. These wicked people are the opposite of the Psalmist. Where the Psalmist is close to

God, listening to God with open obedience and hoping in God's promises, the scheming enemies are far away from God, from God's laws even though they are near to the Psalmist. His enemies are only after mischief and troublemaking, not for the things of God.

Yet as near as his enemies are, the Psalmist knows that God is even closer. His God is watching over him, to preserve, love and keep him. God's commandments are true, worthy of obedience and trustworthy. God is near, He is true and the Psalmist is safe. This loving and living God sees His servants under oppression and burdens and draws even closer to them to give them aid, assistance, comfort and encouragement. No wonder the Psalmist is keen to be obedient to his Worthy God.

In verse 152, we get the idea that the Psalmist, The Psalmist, is now an old man when writing this. Long ago in his youth, when he wrote about in the second stanza, he learnt God's word and the stories, commandments, testimonies of God and those who followed God.

The Psalmist built upon this rock, this established base and is still seeking earnestly to live a life of utter obedience to this living God – a living God who does not and cannot change even if he, the servant Psalmist, has changed as he has grown older. God's relationship with the Psalmist is transforming the Psalmist. WOW!

This should be a huge encouragement to us. How is our prayer life? Is it only on Sundays during church that we seek to connect with God? This God we pray to, seek to worship and obey, is worthy of our attention all day, every day. Are you burdened with something and feeling weighed down? Then ask and implore your God to take your burden, give you extra strength and vitality. He is true. He has promised. He will do it, if you allow Him to.

Pray in the morning and the evening. Worship Him with a life of obedience to Him. Pray with your Bible open and let Him speak to you through it. The Bible is trustworthy and so is the God who gave it. There will be times if you are in a busy work situation when it is pretty well impossible to keep your mind on the things of the Lord. In those situations it is fundamentally important to have stored up your time with the Lord so that you are sure that he will not forget you even when, momentarily, you have forgotten him.

Stanza 20. Resh

(Dave Roberts)

[153] Look on my suffering and deliver me,

for I have not forgotten your law.

[154] Defend my cause and redeem me;

preserve my life according to your promise.

[155] Salvation is far from the wicked,

for they do not seek out your decrees.

[156] Your compassion, LORD, is great;

preserve my life according to your laws.

[157] Many are the foes who persecute me,

but I have not turned from your statutes.

[158] I look on the faithless with loathing,

for they do not obey your word.

[159] See how I love your precepts;

preserve my life, LORD, in accordance with your love.

[160] All your words are true;

all your righteous laws are eternal.

Once again the Psalmist is in danger of losing his life. He is seeking to be delivered from his pains and rescued. He is one of God's servants and seeks to show that by remembering God's law, God's words and behaving as one of God's servants, devoted in fear, reverence and love of Almighty God. And because he hasn't forgotten God's law, he pleads for God to consider and remember him. He is not so distracted by his own problems, that he has forgotten the beauty of God and God's Law. He is faithful to God, because he knows that God is faithful to him.

His persecutors are surrounding him, circling with menace so the Psalmist asks for his God to be his advocate, his redeemer. The Psalmists enemies are spouting lies, ensnaring, oppressing and threatening him, so he calls for his advocate and defender. He also asks that his Almighty God preserve him according to God's own promise. He knows that God always fulfils his promises to those who follow him. The promises of God are as a soft healing balm to the frustrations and wounds of the Psalmist.

And while the Psalmist has a hope in his God, those who persecute, oppress and endanger him are bound for destruction. These wicked oppressors can never find salvation because they are removed from God, ignore

God's decrees and commit blasphemous acts in defiance of God's decrees. The Psalmist's persecutors are only interested in their own wisdom instead of seeking the wisdom of God.

In contrast to these wicked people, the Psalmist has not strayed from God's righteous statutes. He knows Almighty God is compassionate, a great help in times of trouble and preserver of life – nothing can happen to the Psalmist unless God allows it, and God won't do that because of His tremendous promises found in His Law.

The mercies of the Lord endure forever and ever - they are innumerable, immeasurable, immense, tender and true. When he sees the wicked persecuting oppressors disavowing God, actively being wicked in disobedience, the Psalmist is full of righteous indignation and loathing. In contrast to the unrighteous who are against him, the Psalmist loves God's precepts, commands and Law. He knows that the Lord's anger is slow to burn and that the Lord is quick to love those who actively follow him. All of God's words are true! More than that, all of God's laws are righteous, exclaims the Psalmist. All of them from beginning to end and from top to bottom. This was a man willing to stand up for God with zeal, passion and righteous indignation – even if it cost him his very life.

How are you doing in your appreciation for what God has done for you? How are you doing when the world around through the media or people you know, seek to discredit your Christian belief in Almighty God? Are you sometimes filled with zealous indignation when Christians and Christianity attacked in the media or in your workplace? Who is your advocate before God that defends you, wants to redeem you, deliver you from your enemies and those who would seek to bring you down and cause you to lose heart? As Christians, Jesus Christ is our advocate before God the Father. Do you know the promises of God, which can be found in the Bible?

Read the Bible and when praying, have your Bible open and tell God what you are reading. All of Scripture, the Old Testament and the New Testament, is reliable and true - from beginning to end – just as the Psalmist exclaims for the portion that he had at the time. If you do this you will develop an intimacy with God the Father, through God the Son in the power of God the Holy Spirit who lives inside you.

This will develop a love for all of the Bible and not just your favourite parts. Be prepared to worship God in all manner of styles and not just your favourite style.

Yet sometimes we have those in the church who like to discourage and hyper-criticize. No need to go far to find other Christians espousing misleading words against us – particularly in the area of worship. Too many Christians today are being one-dimensional in their acts of church worship, short in their bible reading and living stunted Christian lives because of it.

Just because another person experiences the Holy Spirit in a way different to you, doesn't invalidate that way, but rather reflects the unique way God the Holy Spirit is working in the life of that person. Rejoice when that other person is worshipping Almighty God, even if the style of worship is not your own particular choice. Don't restrict the Holy Spirit's activity in your own life and do not grieve Him by trying to restrict and criticise His activity in another Christian's life – to do so is blasphemous and to call unclean that which is clean.

Go and rejoice in the freedom of the Gospel for all people to worship in Spirit and truth and in many different styles – reflecting the manifold mercies of an ever-gracious God. A God who is gracious to save and merciful to be worshipped and adored, a jealous God worthy of zealous followers. All that arises from the situation the Psalmist was in. It seems to have been a very antagonistic and dangerous one. Fortunately, most of us do not have to live and work in environments quite like that. Although all that the Psalmist says about the non-believers that surrounded him are also true of those who surround us it is often best, both for us and the Gospel, to live, think and act in less antagonistic ways than some of the things the Psalmist said would seem to suggest.

Peter emphasises this in 1 Peter 3:9 - 'Do not repay evil with evil or insult with insult. On the contrary, repay evil with blessing, because to this you were called so that you may inherit a blessing.' That is good New Testament truth and may be more appropriate in our lives and environments than some of the things the Psalmist seems to suggest – though we do not know how he actually lived but only what his thoughts were.

Stanza 21. Shin

(Dave Roberts)

[161] Rulers persecute me without cause,

but my heart trembles at your word.

[162] I rejoice in your promise

like one who finds great spoil.

[163] I hate and detest falsehood

but I love your law.

[164] Seven times a day I praise you

for your righteous laws.

[165] Great peace have those who love your law,

and nothing can make them stumble.

[166] I wait for your salvation, LORD,

and I follow your commands.

[167] I obey your statutes,

for I love them greatly.

[168] I obey your precepts and your statutes,

for all my ways are known to you.

The Psalmist must have had enemies and persecutors from all walks of life. Here the people that are persecuting him are princes. Princes should protect the innocent and bring justice to the oppressed. Princes should act with honour, decorum and nobility really – but not these ones. No. These princes are out to cause the Psalmist, harm without a justifiable reason.

What is The Psalmist's reaction? Is it to run and hide with fear and trembling from these persecuting princes? No. The Psalmist's fear is not from mere mortal men. The Psalmist's reverent fear is for what God says. He is in awe of God's Word. Mere mortals may harm the body, but only God can harm the soul and therefore the Psalmist may be disheartened by persecution, oppression or injustice but the essential foundations of his life are not affected.

And the reason he is in awe and reverent fear of God's Word is because it gives nourishment to him. He rejoices in the promises found. He has great joy at finding the treasures within God's written word. He values these treasures as more valuable than the spoils of war. The Psalmist fights for truth, battles for justice and feeds his hungry soul on all God's Word – not just his favourite parts. He loathes and abhors lies, perjury and false talk.

They are bitter to him and a total contrast to the sweet honey of the Law and God's written Word. He loves it, feeding from it and gaining strength and nourishment – because it is solid Truth. Because of this nourishment and this Truth, the Psalmist gains strength to be at prayerful praise during the day. This perfect God he sought to praise perfectly. When his persecutors came to mind, the Psalmist turned to praise and sang to the God of truth and salvation.

He wasn't going to let these oppressive princes rob him of the joy of singing praise to his Almighty and righteous God. For he knows that God's laws are righteous and those that love God's law in obedience have great peace. This peace is not faltering as if built on sand. No. This peace is solid, reliable and true because it is based on God and His Law. Perfect peace is for those who love God's Law and Words. Those that love God's Law strive wholeheartedly to walk in obedience to God. When persecution comes, they have perfect peace, given by a God of peace.

Because their peace is based on a God of perfect peace, they will not stumble or fall. While the Law was important and obedience to it produced love of it, it could not provide salvation. Salvation could only come from God and that through grace and grace alone.

Because he was assured of salvation, the Psalmist sought to show it by being obedient to God's commands and laws. This love he has for God's statues, testimonies and precepts is a result of his great God saving, rescuing and redeeming him from all his enemies.

The Psalmist, obeyed God's statutes because he loved his God and therefore loved to obey his every command. He strove to show his love for his God by being obedient to Him. His outer life which people saw was a reflection of his inner spiritual life.

Despite the traumas, tribulations and tests that came his way, the Psalmist knew that his salvation was assured, because his God had promised him and God always keeps his promises. The Psalmist knows the mind of God through reading, studying, digesting and loving God's written word – it is the basis for his life of obedience to God.

How are you doing? How are you coping when the tests and rigours of life in the twenty first century come knocking on your day and wanting to disrupt you? Are you concentrating on them and worrying about them? Are they debilitating and corrupting you? What about when people persecute you, lie about you and betray you? How should you react? We are to be like the Psalmist and be at peace. If you are a Christian, you have an intercessor before God the Father and you have the Holy Spirit as a comforter living inside you. That intercessor is God the Son, Jesus Christ, the perfect Prince of peace.

Unlike the rulers and civil servants (the bureaucrats were as much a nuisance in those days as they are today.) who were persecuting the Psalmist, this Prince of Peace gives perfect peace to those who follow Him. Cast your cares, burdens, and worries upon Him and let Him handle them. Let Him give you wisdom to deal and battle with those that seek to persecute you.

Read what God has said in the Bible, follow it and obey it. Obedience, is not a means to salvation, because salvation can only be through God's gift of grace and that grace alone. Obedience to Almighty God is in order to reflect your inner peace with Him. Jesus said, "Love God and love others, for all the Law is summed up in these 2 commandments" (Matthew 22:37-40).

Work out your salvation, as the Psalmist did, with reverent fear. Acknowledge God in all areas of your life and allow the Prince of peace to give you peace – peace in you, with you, on you and spreading out to all the world from you. Seek the treasures in the Bible that are waiting for you to discover. God is trustworthy, faithful and true. Don't just read your favourite passages, but all 66 books. It is worth it because your relationship with God develops and just as the Psalmist is changing for the glory of God, so will your own life.

Stanza 22. Taw

(Dave Roberts)

[169] May my cry come before you, LORD;
give me understanding according to your word.
[170] May my supplication come before you;
deliver me according to your promise.
[171] May my lips overflow with praise,
for you teach me your decrees.
[172] May my tongue sing of your word,
for all your commands are righteous.
[173] May your hand be ready to help me,
for I have chosen your precepts.
[174] I long for your salvation, LORD,
and your law gives me delight.
[175] Let me live that I may praise you,
and may your laws sustain me.
[176] I have strayed like a lost sheep.
Seek your servant,
for I have not forgotten your commands.

The Psalmist continues to the very end of his great poem in verse 170, making requests and seeking deliverance from the dangers and perils of his life. It seems that the Psalmist often faced great dangers throughout his life. His God always delivered him from evil, because God honours his promises to those who are serving Him.

And now in verse 171, he is overflowing with praise. He is effervescent with praise, overflowing, bubbling over and ecstatic with joy for His God. The reason for this exuberance is that he wants to be filled with heavenly wisdom as taught through the decrees and statutes of Almighty God and probably feels that he is well on the way to this great goal.

We get the sense of a spontaneous outburst of praise just exploding from the Psalmist like spring water bubbling from desert sands. Having been taught by the Lord in the practise of righteous obedience to the Law, the Psalmist is intent on teaching others. He is passing on to others, the wisdom he has learned and received. The sense here is of corporate singing of exultant praises of God. Continuing, the Psalmist entreats God to help personally – not my friends or your friends, O God – but you and you alone. Give me your hand O Lord and I will be rescued.

Friends may let me down, discourage and betray me – but you O great God will never do that. Personally save me, the Psalmist is crying. By choosing God's precepts, the Psalmist has dedicated himself to obeying his God and following Him closely.

The Psalmist was keen to be found in full obedience to his God. He yearned to receive full salvation from his God – he had tasted it in part before but he was waiting for it to be complete, as if in expectation of some form of greater salvation. He had been saved from his enemies, those who betrayed him and from wild animals. His present salvation was assured as God had promised him, but so was a future salvation, a salvation of his soul. Hence, we read of his longing to delight in all of God's words and works. All that he has received from the Lord has sustained and helped the Psalmist. Seeing God at work in his life has given him a hope that promised of a future praising God for all God has done, is doing and will continue to do. God's laws have helped the Psalmist to live an obedient life and a life close to God, walking and talking with Him.

Then finally, we have the climax of the Psalm. There is an urgent need to be fulfilled. The lost sheep needs to be found, to be preserved and to be delivered. For all his knowledge of Scripture, his obedience to God and the effect that has had on his own developed righteousness – the Psalmist knows that it was only because God had promised to find him that he would be saved. He was relying on God to assure him of the salvation of his soul. He knew that if a sheep was lost, it was shepherd's job to find that sheep and restore it to the fold.

So he uses this analogy, to symbolise his need of God's salvation. His own righteousness and obedience to the Law couldn't save his soul – only God could do that. God would seek him, find him and restore him. Here he recognizes his need to be a servant of God and wants God to find him. He recognizes he needs to be obedient to God in response to being saved by God's grace and mercy.

How about you? How are you doing in regards to your praise? Is praise bubbling from you like water from a living stream? Are you being fully reliant on God alone for the salvation of your soul and not trusting in your own righteousness, obedience or strength? God is who saves you. God and God alone. God – undivided, unconstrained, uninhibited by our words or anything else. What is your delight, your ultimate delight? Your delight should be in being guided by God in every facet of your life and being in a devoted obedient relationship with Him. Ask Him and he will help. Raise your hand and ask for help, just as Peter did when sinking in the water he tried to walk on, and Jesus rescued him. In response to this grace and the salvation that you can be completely sure of go and live a life of obedience to God – wherever that takes you as His servant.

Conclusion

(Dave Roberts)

As a way of concluding, let us take a look at what some wise people have said about this Psalm and see what further insights they offer us into this magnificent Psalm – John Calvin, Charles Spurgeon and CS Lewis.

John Calvin - "Two things which the prophet mainly aims at; the exhorting of the children of God to follow godliness and a holy life; and the prescribing of the rule, and pointing out the form of the true worship of God, so that the faithful may devote themselves wholly to the study of the Law. Along with these he frequently blends promises for the purpose of animating the worshippers of God to live more justly and piously; and, at the same time, he introduces complaints respecting the impious contempt of the Law, lest they should become tainted by bad examples." (*Calvin's Commentaries, Vol. 11: Psalms, Part IV*, tr. by John King, [1847-50], http://www.sacred-texts.com/chr/calvin/cc11/cc11027.htm) (Accessed 22 April 2015)

Charles Spurgeon - "This Psalm is a wonderful composition. Its expressions are many as the waves, but its testimony is one as the sea. It deals all along with one subject only; but although it consists of a considerable number of verses, some of which are very similar to others, yet throughout its one hundred and seventy-six verses the self-same thought is not repeated: there is always a shade of difference, even when the colour of the thought appears to be the same. … I admire in this psalm the singular commingling of testimony, prayer, and praise. In one verse the Psalmist bears witness; in a second verse he praises; in a third verse he prays. It is an incense made up of many spices; but they are wonderfully compounded and worked together, so as to form one perfect sweetness. The blending greatly increases the value of the whole. You would not like to have one-third of the psalm composed of prayer — marked up to the sixtieth verse, for instance; and then another part made up exclusively of praise; and yet a third portion of unmixed testimony. It is best to have all these divinely-sweet ingredients intermixed, and wrought into a sacred unity, as you have them in this thrice-hallowed psalm. Its prayers bear testimony, and its testimonies are fragrant with praise. " (Charles Spurgeon: Psalm 119, Zion Christian Press.

http://zionchristianpress.org/spurgeon/golden_alphabet

/index.html) (Accessed 22 April 2015)

CS Lewis - "Everyone has probably noticed that from the literary or technical point of view, it is the most formal and elaborate of them all. The technique consists in taking a series of words which are all, for purposes of this poem, more or less synonyms, and ringing the changes on them through each of its eight-verse sections – which themselves correspond to the letter of the alphabet. In other words, this poem is not, and does not pretend to be, a sudden outpouring of the heart like, say, Psalm 18. It is a pattern, a thing done like embroidery, stitch by stitch, through long, quiet hours, for love of the subject and for the delight in leisurely, disciplined craftsmanship. Now this, in itself, seems to me very important because it lets us into the mind and mood of the poet. We can guess at once that he felt about the Law somewhat as he felt about his poetry; both involved exact and loving conformity to an intricate pattern." (CS Lewis, Reflections on the Psalms, p58, Harcourt Book, 1958)

A friend of mine, Sharona Wilson told me a fond memory she has about Psalm 119. "Years ago, I gave my boss a Bible. He had been telling me that he had never owned anything but a KJV and didn't understand it at all. I gave him a hardback NIV pew Bible. He put it in his desk drawer but never looked at it. One day I went into his office to find him shuffling through the pages of the Bible, clearly looking for something. I asked if I could help and he told me he had been watching a football game and someone held up a sign that said "John 3:16" so he was trying to find out what it said. I helped him find the verse. Then he closed the Bible, opened it at random and read aloud, "Your word is a lamp to my feet and a light for my path" and I said "Psalm 119:105."

He looked at me in shock, and with sheer admiration in his voice said, "Oh, you're good." Then he closed the Bible, opened it at random and said "Let's try again." Then he read a verse I had no idea where it came from, but it sounded a bit like it could have been Isaiah. I said tentatively, "Isaiah?" He said, "No, think bullfrog…" And I said "Oh, Jeremiah." and we both had a laugh about that. OK, it's random, but I have a laugh about that every time I think of that happening, him thinking I was such a brilliant biblical scholar, because I knew a verse from Psalm 119. "

Let's sum up what each of these witnesses for Psalm 119 offer us in the twenty first century. For Calvin, the Psalm encourages followers of God to follow godliness, live and study diligently what God has revealed. He also notes how the Psalmist frequently blends promises in order to animate worshippers of God to live more justly and humbly.

For Spurgeon, it portrays a sacred unity, whereby prayers, testimony and praise intermingle, and form sweet perfumed incense. Psalm 119's prayers bear testimony, and its testimonies are fragrant with praise. For CS Lewis it was like an intricate embroidery, patterned, cunningly weaved and a labour of love for Almighty God and His Law.

What is it for you? Have you considered scripture as being like an elaborately intricate staircase to ascend? Does it animate you? Are you enthralled by the intricacy of its design so that you can get to know your God more, in order to live a life worthy of him as your prayers bear testimony and your testimonies of God's goodness bear the fruit of praise?

Hopefully as we are now at the end of this little book, you will have found a new delight in reading your Bible: all 66 books of it including perhaps some that you have never read before and sometimes just hearing from your wonderful Lord. Ask yourself how you view the Bible, how you read it, why you read it and do you listen to God speaking to you as you do so? Has your attitude and feelings changed towards the Bible as a whole? Do certain parts of the Bible now captivate you more than they did before? I do hope and pray so.

About Partakers

Vision Statement: Partakers exists to communicate and disseminate resources for the purposes of Christian Discipleship, Evangelism and Worship by employing radical and relevant methods, including virtual reality and online distribution.

Mission Statement: Helping the world, one person at a time, to engage in whole life discipleship, as Partakers of Jesus Christ.

info@partakers.co.uk
www.partakers.co.uk

14899457R00089

Printed in Great Britain
by Amazon.co.uk, Ltd.,
Marston Gate.